the official

RANGERS ANNUAL 2004

Written by
Douglas Russell

g

A Grange Publication

© 2003. Published by Grange Communications Ltd., Edinburgh, under licence from Rangers Football Club. Printed in the EU.

With thanks to Paul Geddes and Fiona Smith of Rangers Retail Department and Rangers photographer, Lynne Norris

ISBN 1 902704 48 7

£5.99

Contents

player of the year

To all friends of Rangers, it came as no surprise when team captain Barry Ferguson was honoured with the Player of the Year award at the Scottish Players' Union annual event in late April 2003. Less than one month later, it was a case of two-in-a-row when he landed the Scottish Football Writers' Association Player of the Year title for the second time in only four seasons, joining an elite group of just four other footballers (Henrik Larsson, Brian Laudrup, Sandy Jardine and John Greig) who have won this title on two occasions. He had, in truth, been simply immense throughout all three domestic campaigns in Season 2002/03 as the 'Light Blues' hit the silver trail of glory. Additionally, only top scorer Ronald de Boer (with twenty) bettered the Scot's goal tally of eighteen.

Barry Ferguson had lifted his first-ever trophy as Rangers skipper in March 2002 when Ayr United were beaten 4-0 in the CIS Insurance League Cup final at Hampden. Despite carrying a long term rib injury, the player

(a product of the Ibrox youth policy) had been quite mesmerising that spring afternoon at the National Stadium and netted his side's crucial second goal into the bargain. Although he had been just as convincing in the Old Firm semi-final clash of the same competition the previous month, it was another encounter with the team in green and white hoops that earned him a place in Ibrox folklore – the Scottish Cup final of 2002.

Even those of a more neutral persuasion had to admit that Barry's total domination of the midfield that memorable day was the very stuff of legend. Of course, there was also the SMALL matter of a stunning free-kick goal that was good enough to grace any European Cup final! The young man had become, as David Murray commented at the time, a really big player and captain for Rangers.

Last season, this quality of play was evident game to game – with, for good measure, the additional bonus

BARRY Ferguson

of some important goals. After claiming his first SPL goal of the 2002/03 campaign in the Easter Road destruction of Hibernian (4-2, 18.8.02), Ferguson made it three-in-a-row with strikes in both the Ibrox clash with Aberdeen (2-0, 25.8.02) and the East End Park encounter with Dunfermline (6-0, 1.9.02). Two September goals away to Livingston (2-0, 14.9.02) and Dundee United (3-0, 28.9.02) were followed by a double in the rather comprehensive 6-1 Govan crushing of Kilmarnock in late October. From a goals point of view, his hat-trick in the pre-Christmas 3-0 victory over Dundee United must definitely be mentioned.

Of course, his hands were on another trophy in March 2003 when old friends Celtic were beaten 2-1 at the National Stadium in the CIS Insurance Cup final but he had to wait a little longer (until May 25th to be precise) to take hold of the one that really mattered! After a day of high drama at both Ibrox and Rugby Park (where Celtic

were playing), Barry's delight was there for all to see as he proudly held aloft the rather heavy SPL trophy amidst scenes of unbelievable joy both on and off the park. One week later at the National Stadium, the season was complete (in more ways than one) with the third piece of domestic silverware after Dundee were beaten in the Scottish Cup final.

It should not be forgotten that Barry Ferguson was Scotland's Player of the Year for Season 2002/03 despite not being 100% fit for much of the campaign. No wonder he is already a legend down Govan way.

team Rangers

the manager

alex MCLEISH

By the end of Season 2002/03, manager Alex McLeish had achieved legendary status in the eyes of the fans after leading Rangers to a domestic treble (the club's seventh in total) of SPL Championship and both the Scottish and CIS Cups. Astonishingly, the league title was number 50 for the club – a world record. McLeish followed in the footsteps of previous managers Bill Struth, Scott Symon, Jock Wallace, Walter Smith and Dick Advocaat who had all achieved this marvellous feat of total domestic success back in Seasons 1948/49, 1963/64, 1975/76, 1977/78, 1992/93 and 1998/99. In addition, since succeeding Advocaat at the Ibrox helm some eighteen months previously, Alex McLeish (Bank of Scotland Manager of the Year for Season 2002/03) was unbeaten in eight Hampden cup visits.

Maurice Ross

Making twenty-two starts for the 'Light Blues' in Season 2002/03, the young Dundee-born, right-sided defender scored his first-ever Rangers goal when Livingston were beaten 2-0 at the City Stadium in mid September last term. Although his last SPL appearance of the campaign was in the early April 2-0 Ibrox victory over John Lambie's Partick Thistle, Ross was a second half substitute (for Michael Mols) on Scottish Cup Final Day when the Hampden game was still evenly balanced at 0-0. The speedy youngster is one of the most promising Scottish footballers in the country.

Kevin Muscat

Now in his second season with Rangers, the Australian international full-back arrived at Ibrox from Molyneux (the home of Wolverhampton Wanderers) in the summer of 2002 under freedom of contract. Although his name did not appear in the starting line-up for any of the five Old Firm clashes with Celtic last term, the unyielding Muscat made a total of twenty-six league and cup starts in that wonderful treble year.

Fernando Ricksen

Only two first-team players (Stefan Klos and Barry Ferguson) made more starts than Fernando Ricksen in the period that was 2002/03. Whether positioned in midfield or at right full-back, the versatile Dutchman (now a regular for his country) grew in stature as the season progressed, amassing a total of forty-five games with the added bonus of three goals in the SPL encounters with Dunfermline (6-0, 1.9.02) and Hearts (4-0, 1.12.02). Fernando's crucial double at Tynecastle in the latter fixture (when he netted the first and third goals of the Sunday afternoon's entertainment) helped ensure that Rangers stayed just one point behind leaders Celtic at that stage of the championship race.

Michael Ball

Although he missed all of last season through injury, Michael Ball (one full England cap in addition to honours at both under-18 and under-21 levels) is now thankfully back playing for the club again. Certainly the Ibrox fans were delighted to see him celebrating on the park with the rest of the team at the end of that famous May Day when the SPL Championship came back to Govan. After the Scottish Cup triumph at Hampden, manager Alex McLeish confirmed that the player (Rangers' second most expensive signing at £6.5 million) had only just missed out being part of the squad for that game.

Robert Malcolm

Partnering either Craig Moore or Lorenzo Amoruso to great and determined effect at different times throughout the various 2002/03 competitions, Bob Malcolm (who rarely misplaces a pass) began twenty-six games wearing the light blue. At Dens Park in early November, when he was a replacement for the injured Amoruso and lined up beside Craig Moore at the heart of the Rangers defence, the solid stopper gave his side an all-important first-half lead before the eventual 3-0 league victory over Jim Duffy's Dundee.

Zurab Khizanishvili

Despite interest from both Sporting Lisbon and Everton for his signature, the cultured Georgian international (a close friend of Shota Arveladze) joined Rangers on a three year deal in the summer of 2003. Earlier, when the talented defender had first arrived in Scotland to play for Dundee, top clubs such as Ajax, West Ham and Fulham were also chasing him. He made his dark blue debut away to Aberdeen in April 2001. After suffering a serious knee injury in a game with Celtic, the youngster fought his way back to full fitness and enjoyed an extensive first-team run on Tayside in Season 2002/03. The culmination of that period was an impressive late May display at the heart of the Dundee defence on Scottish Cup final day despite the fact that he was given the extremely difficult task of marking Ronald de Boer. Zurab Khizanishvili is a footballer in the true sense of the word.

Stephen Hughes

The young midfielder (now under contract until at least year 2007) was quite excellent in the games with Kilmarnock (4-0, 11.5.03) and Hearts (2-0, 18.5.03) as Rangers pushed for SPL glory in the early summer of 2003. Although Stephen only made the starting line-up seven times last season, he claimed Rangers fourth of the afternoon when, appearing as substitute for captain Barry Ferguson late-on, a December trip to the Tynecastle district of Scotland's capital ended with four goals and three SPL points.

Shota Arveladze

Known as Showtime Shota during his time with Ajax in Holland (where he hit thirty-seven goals in one season), the Georgian international delighted the Ibrox crowd with an impromptu display of disco dancing following the presentation of the SPL trophy in late May. Third top-scorer at the club last season after Ronald de Boer and Barry Ferguson, Arveladze (who, believe it or not, is a descendent of a Georgian king!) netted fifteen times in thirty starts with goals in both the first and final SPL games against Kilmarnock (1-1, 3.8.02) and Dunfermline (6-1, 25.5.03) respectively. Part of his season's tally was a double in the Tannadice Dundee United clash (4-1, 13.4.03) and an earlier hat-trick when pre-Christmas visitors Livingston were beaten 4-3 on a cold December evening in Govan.

Peter Lovenkrands
The Danish winger repeated his final feat of May 2002 when he scored the winner at Hampden against Celtic in March 2003 as Rangers secured the first part of their treble success courtesy of the CIS Insurance Cup. Earlier in the same competition, he also claimed the winner but this time at Easter Road when Hibernian fell 3-2 despite scoring first. With injury unfortunately playing a part in his season, Lovenkrands still began twenty-seven games and netted twelve times. In the third SPL game of last term he was really quite awesome, scoring twice as well as making another and winning his side's penalty in a 4-2 Sunday outing to the (rather wet) Leith district of Edinburgh. Once again, during the latter Hibernian game, the travelling fans applauded his trademark gymnastic celebrations.

Steven Thompson
Having arrived at Rangers from Dundee United at the turn of the year (as Billy Dodds headed in the opposite direction), the striker scored on his Light Blue debut when, late-on in the early January 2003 Ibrox game with Dundee, he slotted home a de Boer cutback to seal a 3-1 SPL victory. Although he only made the starting line-up once last season (2-0 v Motherwell, 19.3.03), two of his substitute appearances were decidedly important to the club. Firstly, at Hampden on Scottish Cup semi-final day, his second-half presence in the Motherwell game was a major factor in the game turning Rangers way and secondly, his goal against Dunfermline during the last SPL fixture of the season was crucial for obvious reasons, in addition to being number 100 of the league campaign.

Henning Berg
Norway's captain and most-capped defender, Henning Berg signed a one year deal in the summer of 2003. The big Scandinavian had a marvellous 2002/03 season with English Premiership outfit Blackburn Rovers before arriving at Ibrox and has played under Kenny Dalglish, Sir Alex Ferguson and Graeme Souness during his years in the English Premiership.

Paoli Vanoli
The left-sided Italian defender joined the club at the same time as Henning Berg and made his Rangers debut (as a substitute for Michael Ball) in the opening SPL game of the season when Kilmarnock were beaten 4-0 at Ibrox. Having played at the highest level in Italy's Serie A with the likes of Parma, Vanoli will obviously be an invaluable addition to Alex McLeish's squad.

Michael Mols

Making the starting line-up for the first time last season in the late October clash with Kilmarnock at Ibrox, the Dutch hitman netted twice in the 6-1 demolition of the Ayrshire outfit. Another three doubles were recorded in the games with Aberdeen (2-1, 1.2.03), Partick Thistle (2-0, 5.4.03) and Kilmarnock (4-0, 11.5.03) before Mols scored the all-important opener (in just three minutes) against Dunfermline at home on Championship Day in late May. His total for Season 2002/03 was fourteen goals in thirty starts for Rangers. Interestingly enough, all of the goals were scored within the Glasgow city boundary – twelve at Ibrox and one at both Firhill and Hampden. Deciding to extend his stay with the club, the player signed a new one year contract with Rangers in June 2003.

Nuno Capucho

The first of Rangers 2003 summer signings, the attacking international (thirty-four caps for Portugal) arrived at the club on a two-year deal after having spent six years with Porto, his country's 2002/03 league champions. Although the right-winger was used only sparingly by coach Jose Mourinho last season, Capucho was part of the side that defeated Celtic in the Seville final of the UEFA Cup tournament in May. Back in October 2001, the player (socks at ankles) had been hugely impressive when Porto turned up the Champions League heat on Celtic in their 3-0 home victory. Following the confirmation that Capucho was a Rangers player, Alex McLeish was quoted saying 'In the past couple of years, Porto have done very well and he has been at the heart of their success. He is a brave player and there is plenty of skill about his game.' As a youngster in 1991, the forward was a member of the Portugese team that won the FIFA World Youth Championship.

Michel Arteta

The young Spanish midfielder (ex Barcelona) claimed his first-ever goal for Rangers when Dunfermline were crushed 6-0 at Ibrox in early September last season. He scored another four (in thirty-four starts) during the 2002/03 Treble campaign, the most famous of which was surely that crucial penalty, his team's sixth goal of the game, on the last day of the league season when the Championship was finally won. In the opening SPL encounter of this season, Arteta capped a marvellous 'Man of the Match' per-formance with two goals (one, a first-half penalty and the other, a stunning twenty-five yard drive in the second period) when visi-tors Kilmarnock were on the receiving end of a comprehensive 4-0 defeat.

11

the Honours

Scottish League Championships
(50 in total)

1891, 1899, 1900, 1901, 1902,
1911, 1912, 1913, 1918, 1920,
1921, 1923, 1924, 1925, 1927,
1928, 1929, 1930, 1931, 1933,
1934, 1935, 1937, 1939, 1947,
1949, 1950, 1953, 1956, 1957,
1959, 1961, 1963, 1964, 1975,
1976, 1978, 1987, 1989, 1990,
1991, 1992, 1993, 1994, 1995,
1996, 1997, 1999, 2000, 2003.

Scottish Cups
(31)

1894, 1897, 1898, 1903, 1928,
1930, 1932, 1934, 1935, 1936,
1948, 1949, 1950, 1953, 1960,
1962, 1963, 1964, 1966, 1973,
1976, 1978, 1979, 1981, 1992,
1993, 1996, 1999, 2000, 2002,
2003.

Scottish League Cups
(23)

1946/47, 1948/49, 1960/61,
1961/62, 1963/64, 1964/65,
1970/71, 1975/76, 1977/78,
1978/79, 1981/82, 1983/84,
1984/85, 1986/87, 1987/88,
1988/89, 1990/91, 1992/93,
1993/94, 1996/97, 1998/99,
2001/02, 2002/03.

European Cup Winners' Cup

Winners 1972
Runners up 1961, 1967.

The Victory Cup

1946

HEADLINE NEWS

RANGERS MADE THE FOLLOWING FOOTBALL HEADLINES DURING SEASON 2002/03.

What was the occassion? The clue is in the date!

1 'DE BOER ON HAND TO OFFSET AN UPSET'
Sunday Times, 23.2.03

2 'BY ECK THAT WAS TOUGH'
Sunday Mirror, 20.4.03

3 'REIGN CLAUDS GATHER AT IBROX'
Daily Record, 12.9.02

4 'CAPTAIN CONQUERING HEARTS AND MINDS'
Daily Mail, 17.2.03

5 'MOORE WILL MISS THE IBROX HEART OF GOLD'
Daily Mail, 2.6.0

6 'CLINICAL RANGERS BREEZE THROUGH'
Sunday Times, 26.1.03

7 'THOUSANDS ARE LEFT CRYING FOR MOF'
Daily Mail, 12.5

8 'BLUE-EYED BOY'
Daily Mail, 13.5.03

9 'IT ONLY TAKES A MINUTE TO WIN IT'
Daily Mail, 26.5.03

10 'McLEISH CARVES HIS NAME IN HISTORY'
Sunday Times, 1.6.03

FROM THE
trophy room

KATOWICE BLACK VASE 1988

When Graeme Souness was at the helm as manager, Season 1987/88 was the only year that Rangers failed to win the Scottish League Championship. The Ibrox club, therefore, participated in the 1988/89 UEFA Cup competition and were drawn against the powerful GKS Katowice of Poland in the first-round.

Although Rangers won the first-leg 1-0 at Ibrox (a Mark Walters goal), the impressive Eastern Europeans were most unfortunate not to return home with at least a draw after a notable display of attacking football in Glasgow. That night, many of the 40,000 plus crowd reckoned Rangers would be in for an extremely difficult time when the teams met again in Poland one month later. After all, their Govan visitors had created several good chances in the opening ninety minutes of the initial clash.

As if to confirm the worst of fears, Katowice's Furtok scored after just five minutes of the return leg. It was then the turn of Terry Butcher to take centre stage and the Rangers captain struck twice (with headed goals) to give his side a 2-1 half-time lead. Although the Poles equalised through Kubisztal just after the hour mark, subsequent goals from both Ians (Durrant and Ferguson) meant that Rangers recorded an impressive 4-2 away win and were through to the next round of the competition.

Made entirely of coal, this stunning black vase was presented to Rangers by the officials of GKS Katowice.

first leg
7.9.88

Rangers 1   Katowice 0
(Walters)

Rangers: Woods, Stevens, Brown, Gough, Wilkins, Butcher, Drinkell, Ferguson, Cooper, Durrant and Walters.

second leg
5.10.88

Katowice 2   Rangers 4
(Butcher 2, Ferguson, Durrant.)

Rangers: Woods, Stevens, Munro, Gough, Wilkins, Butcher, Cooper, Ferguson, McCoist, Durrant and Walters.

FROM THE
trophy room

EUROPEAN CUP WINNERS' CUP CAMPAIGN PENNANTS 1971/72

first round

1st LEG
RENNES 1   RANGERS 1
Johnston (68)

2nd LEG
RANGERS 1   RENNES 0
MacDonald (38)

second round

1st LEG
RANGERS 3
SPORTING LISBON 2
Stein (9, 19), Henderson (28)

2nd LEG
SPORTING LISBON 4
RANGERS 3
Stein (27, 46), Henderson (100)

*After extra-time,
Rangers won on the 'away goals' rule

quarter-final

1st LEG
TORINO 1   RANGERS 1
Johnston (12)

2nd LEG
RANGERS 1   TORINO 0
MacDonald (46)

semi-final

1st LEG
BAYERN MUNICH 1
RANGERS 1
Zobel og (49)

2nd LEG
RANGERS 2
BAYERN MUNICH 0
Jardine (1) Parlane (23)

final

**NOU CAMP STADIUM, BARCELONA
MAY 24, 1972. ATTENDANCE 35,000**

RANGERS 3   MOSCOW DYNAMO 2
Stein (24), Johnston (40, 49)

*RANGERS: McCloy, Jardine, Mathieson, Greig, Johnstone,
Smith, McLean, Conn, Stein, MacDonald and Johnston.*

theoldfirm
LEAGUE CUP FINAL

When Rangers lined-up against Celtic in the March 2003 final of the League Cup, it was the 12th time that the Old Firm had met at this ultimate stage of the competition. The record books now verify that the 'Light Blues' have lifted the trophy (presently sponsored by CIS Insurance) after eight of these Hampden encounters - twice as many times as their arch rivals from across the city. These are the famous wins:

SEASON 1964/65
Rangers 2 Celtic 1

Inspired by the legendary Jim Baxter, Rangers retained the trophy thanks to a second-half double from centre-forward Jim Forrest who, incidentally, had created a League Cup final record the previous year when netting four times against Morton in the 5-0 triumph. The striker's goal tally of 57 for Season 1964/65 comprised: League Cup - 18, Scottish Cup - 3, League Championship – 30 and European Cup - 6. Not surprisingly, Forrest (whose name was also on both Rangers goals in the 2-1 League Cup semi-final win over Dundee United that September) was club top scorer for the year!

SEASON 1970/71
Rangers 1 Celtic 0

Out jumping Celtic captain Billy McNeill, a very young Derek Johnstone (just 16 years and 355 days old!) was rightly acclaimed when his near legendary, headed goal (from a Willie Johnston cross) was enough to defeat the afternoon's hot favourites on 24th October 1970. Why hot favourites? Well, Celtic had previously won five successive League Cups as well as five successive championships! On this day however, they were famously beaten and the silverware was heading for Govan. It was the Ibrox club's first major trophy in four years (as well as the first under new manager Willie Waddell) and a Hampden crowd of over 106,000 witnessed the occasion.

SEASON 1975/76
Rangers 1 Celtic 0

A second-half flying header from Alex MacDonald ignited the blue touch-paper at one end of Hampden. This goal from the combative midfielder (and true blue Rangers man) confirmed part one of a trio of triumphs that season and, by early May, manager Jock Wallace's side had secured a domestic treble including the first-ever Premier Division title.

SEASON 1977/78
Rangers 2 Celtic 1

Extra-time was required when the Old Firm crossed swords again in March 1978. Davie Cooper (with a tremendous volley) and Gordon Smith (with an extra-time header) were on target to ensure part one of another treble celebration - the club's second in three years.

SEASON 1983/84
Rangers 3 Celtic 2

The day belonged to Ally McCoist with the legendary striker claiming a hat-trick in this famous victory. His third goal came in extra-time from the penalty spot after Celtic had equalised in the last minute of the ninety from the spot, with Ally himself having given away the penalty! Rangers had now enjoyed success in this competition a record twelve times.

SEASON 1986/87
Rangers 2   Celtic 1

Another two true-blue legends, Ian Durrant and Davie Cooper (with a late penalty conversion) gave player-manager Graeme Souness (who missed the game through injury) his first major trophy in Scotland. This fiery encounter saw 10 players booked and Maurice Johnston, wearing the green of Celtic, sent off.

SEASON 1990/91
Rangers 2   Celtic 1

Despite defender Elliott giving his side an early second-half lead, subsequent strikes from winger Mark Walters and Richard Gough (in extra-time) ensured a light blue triumph. It was Gough himself who collected the trophy, his first of many as captain of the club.

SEASON 2002/03
Rangers 2   Celtic 1

As with the two previous Old Firm League Cup finals, Rangers are victors on the back of a 2-1 result. Despite sustained second-half pressure from their opponents, first period goals from Argentine Claudio Caniggia and Dane Peter Lovenkrands ensured a glorious Sunday in the sun for those of a blue persuasion at the National Stadium.

Since the first-ever League Cup tournament back in Season 1946/47 (when Rangers were also victorious), this unique piece of silverware has graced the Ibrox trophy room an astonishing twenty-three times. Additionally, since the start of the 1990s, Rangers have lifted the trophy seven times to Celtic's three.

THEY WORE THE BLUE

Few would begrudge the Player of the Year accolades showered upon Barry Ferguson at the end of Season 2002/03. Week in and week out, his performances at the heart of the team were nothing short of sensational even although on many occasions he was far from 100% fit. Over the years, many other midfield maestros have worn the blue and achieved heroic status at the club. Here's a brief look at the careers of three other famous Rangers players whose prowess in Barry's area of the park earned them legendary status in the eyes of the fans.

RAY WILKINS

His stay in Glasgow lasted just two years but Ray Wilkins was considered by many to be the finest midfield talent to don the blue since the genius that was Jim Baxter. Sporting a football pedigree second to none, the Englishman had proudly worn the colours of Chelsea, Manchester United and AC Milan as well as playing for his country no less than eighty-four times. After making his debut in the 3-2 victory over Hearts (28.11.87), Wilkins remained an ever-present in the side for the remainder of that season. He quickly realised the true importance of the Ibrox legions and endeared himself to all 'follow-followers' everywhere by always ushering celebrating players towards them after a goal.

Season 1988/89 had hardly begun before reigning champions Celtic came calling on a gloriously hot, late-August afternoon. That day Ray Wilkins scored what was to be his only league goal of the campaign – that day Ray Wilkins became a Ranger for life. Ten minutes before the break, with the game finely balanced at 1-1, the player pounced on a loose clearance just outside the Celtic penalty area and hit the most perfectly judged and exquisite right-foot volley which screamed past Andrews in goal. Rangers were ahead and would not be caught as a famous 5-1 victory began to unfold.

In due course, the championship returned to Ibrox that season along with the League Cup which was retained. A glorious domestic treble was on the cards but sadly both Ray (and that other influential midfielder Ian Ferguson) missed the Scottish Cup final through injury thus handing a major, pre-match advantage to 1-0 winners Celtic.

Wilkins was an ever-present in the championship race the following season right up until his last game for the club against Dunfermline at Ibrox on 25 November 1989. He had decided to return to London for family reasons. As he stood alone in the centre-circle after the final whistle, a standing ovation from some 40,000 people echoed throughout Govan. Knowing that he would never wear the blue of Rangers again, Ray Wilkins was not the only one to shed a tear.

THEY WORE THE BLUE

IAN DURRANT

Govan lad Ian Durrant joined the only club he ever wanted to play for as a schoolboy. Benefiting from the Rangers training and coaching system, he made his league debut in the April 1985 game with Morton. By the following season, a blossoming Durrant, (now established in the first team) was scoring in his Old Firm debut at Ibrox when Celtic were comprehensively beaten 3-0. With the arrival of Graeme Souness, the No.10 jersey would become his own and the player wore it with pride on 39 league occasions that season as Rangers lifted the championship. The League Cup also returned to the trophy room after Durrant's opening strike set the Light Blues on the road to a 2-1 final victory over Celtic at the National Stadium.

Although the title was not retained in Season 1987/88, the League Cup did remain at Ibrox. Rangers faced Aberdeen at Hampden (October 1987) in what was to become one of the great finals of the modern era. After the team from the north opened the scoring, goals from Davie Cooper (a ferocious free-kick) and Durrant gave Rangers the advantage. Aberdeen then scored twice before striker Robert Fleck's dramatic late, late equaliser. With no further scoring in extra-time, it was down to penalties. Few friends of Rangers will ever forget that famous Durrant pose – motionless with his arms high in a 'Victory V' stance - after he had netted the decisive kick. That priceless image is now part of Ibrox folklore.

Fate dealt the cruellest of blows at Pittodrie (in the third month of the 1988/89 Championship) when Ian's knee was virtually shattered following a quite shocking Neil Simpson tackle. It would be almost three long and painful years before the player pulled on his beloved blue again. On that emotional day at Ibrox in April 1991 (when Hibernian were the visitors), thirty-five thousand people rose as one to greet him like a long lost son, emerging from the darkness into sunlight once again.

Home and abroad, Season 1992/93 was really special for both player and club as Rangers completed a domestic treble in addition to achieving glory on foreign fields. In the intimidating atmosphere of the Velodrome, it was Durrant's stunning equaliser against Marseille that ensured Rangers became the first visitors in fifteen European ties to avoid defeat in this hostile arena. That was the midfielder's third goal in an unforgettable European Cup campaign - his other strikes being the away goal against Danish champions Lyngby and the opener against Bruges of Belgium in the 2-1 March '93 Ibrox victory. The season ended with his Man of the Match award for a peerless performance in the treble-clinching 1993 Scottish Cup final triumph over Aberdeen.

Ian Durrant joined Kilmarnock the season after 'Nine-In-A-Row' had been achieved by the Ibrox club. Even to this day, however, that famous 'blue, white, dynamite' chorus can still be heard down Govan way!

THEY WORE THE BLUE

PAUL GASCOIGNE

There were many raised eyebrows in the summer of 1995 when manager Walter Smith announced that Rangers had completed the signing of wayward genius Paul Gascoigne from Lazio for a fee of over £4million. His football pedigree was never in doubt - it was just the fact that the Geordie had only played 47 games in three Italian seasons, spending a fair percentage of time on the injury list. However, any initial doubts were soon quashed when the player hit a rich vein of form on the park, becoming an instant folk hero to all friends of Rangers.

In his first Glasgow season, Gascoigne netted 19 times in 41 games, including a quite sublime goal in the September 1995 2-0 victory at Celtic Park when he guided the ball past a wrong-footed Marshall after a surging, strength-sapping sixty-yard run. Probably three of his most celebrated strikes came in the championship decider against Aberdeen in late April, with his second that day being rightly judged as one of the finest individual efforts ever seen at Ibrox. Only ten minutes remained (with the score 1-1) when 'Gazza' gathered the ball in his own half and set of on a run, dismissing challenge after Aberdeen challenge before steering a wonderful left-foot shot past Michael Watt in goal. 'Eight-In-A-Row' had become a reality and it came as little surprise when he scooped both Scottish 'Player of the Year' awards shortly after.

Although his name seemed to appear as much on the front pages the following year, there was still much to admire and write about in a football sense. Indeed, it was flashes of his genius that decided the destination of November's League Cup when Rangers met Hearts in the final on a bitterly wet Hampden day. In the second-half, the Gorgie Road side had drawn level, cancelling out an earlier double by Ally McCoist. Step forward Paul Gascoigne to conjure up two moments of magic which put Rangers home and dry – despite the elements! Against the same team just one month later, the Englishman ran the show once again in an emphatic 4-1 Tynecastle victory.

Even although 1996/97 was really the season of Brian Laudrup, Gascoigne played a major part and was there at Tannadice on May 7th for the ultimate triumph of nine glorious years. He never completed another full campaign with the club, making just fourteen league appearances and scoring three goals in 1997/98. It would certainly have been more but for a lengthy suspension following his red card in the November clash with Celtic. He joined Middlesbrough in March 1998 for some £3.5million.

At the end of the day, Paul Gascoigne's contribution to two championships in three seasons will never be forgotten by the Ibrox masses who idolised him during his all-too-brief time in Scotland.

missing word quiz

FILL IN THE NAME OF THE MISSING RANGER FROM THIS SELECTION OF SEASON 2002/03 FOOTBALL HEADLINES. THE CLUE IS IN THE DATE!

1. '_____ SETTING UP RESIDENCE AT HAMPDEN WITH A PERFECT RECORD' 2.6.03.

2. 'SMILES BETTER AS _____ SINKS CELTS' 8.12.02

3. '_____ GETS THE GOAL – FERGUSON GETS THE PRAISE' 30.12.02

4. '_____ DEAD BRILLIANT' 4.11.02

5. 'NEW CALM AND COOL MEANS _____ HAS NOW COLLECTED' 9.11.02

6. 'UNITED DESTROYED BY DELUXE _____' 14.4.03

7. '_____ DANCER' 15.9.02

8. '£7.5MILLION JACKPOT KEEPS _____ AT IBROX' 25.3.03

9. '_____ AN INSTANT HIT' 3.1.03

10. 'HEARTS IN MOUTHS UNTIL _____ NOD' 19.5.03

Answers on page 62

scottish

CUP QUIZ

1. Which side played host to Rangers in the third round of last season's Scottish Cup competition?

2. Who scored for the Light Blues that night?

3. Rangers travelled to Ayr in the next round. Name their ground.

4. Shota Arveladze scored the only goal of the game. True or false?

5. In the fifth round, after Dunfermline had taken the lead at East End Park, who equalised for Rangers?

6. Who was sent-off in the above clash?

7. Who scored his 18th goal of the season in the replay at Ibrox?

8. What was the half-time score in the semi-final against Motherwell at Hampden?

9. Name the player who gave Rangers the lead in the second period of that game?

10. Which three players came on as second-half substitutes in the Scottish Cup final with Dundee?

dutch**of**class

Ronald de Boer

With Rangers and Celtic all square at 1-1 in the second Old Firm clash of last season, Ronald de Boer once again stamped his name on a game in the most dramatic fashion. After a clever reverse pass from Michael Mols had found winger Neil McCann, his subsequent cross into the box was beautifully volleyed home by the Dutchman arriving in the area at speed from midfield. It was a truly magnificent goal with, in truth, de Boer making a difficult chance look easy.

Both Ronald (twice 'Player of the Year' in his homeland) and his twin Frank were vital components of a wondrous Ajax side that dominated the football headlines back in the 1990s. The year 1995 was particularly special to the brothers as their team not only won the domestic title in Holland but also the European Cup, the European Super Cup and the World Club Championship as well! Four years later, in 1999, the de Boers headed for the Nou Camp stadium to join Spanish giants Barcelona with £15million being paid to Ajax for their joint services. Ronald scored on his Barcelona debut and ended the season the proud owner of a prestigious Primera Liga championship medal.

Brought to Scotland by Dick Advocaat in the summer of 2000 for some £4.5million, a whole series of injuries (knee, toe and ankle) blighted the initial and early stages of his Rangers career. Last season, with the player fully fit, the Ibrox masses were treated week after week to the sublime, enthralling skills of a genuine world class footballer. In August 2002, de Boer scored in three consecutive SPL games – the encounters with Dundee (3-0, 10.8.02), Hibernian (4-2., 18.8.02) and Aberdeen (2-0, 25.8.02) and then followed this with doubles in the league match with Partick Thistle (3-0, 21.9.02) and the UEFA Cup clash with Viktoria Zizkov (3-1, 3.10.02).

Another highlight of that early season period came in the first 'Old Firm' tussle when he equalised at Celtic Park (almost immediately after Larsson had given the home side a 2-1 advantage) with a glorious headed goal from McCann's superb cross and then buried himself in the celebrating Rangers fans behind Douglas in goal!

Following his rather special strike when Celtic came calling in early December, Ronald claimed another two important goals in the games with Partick Thistle (2-1, 22.12.02) and Dundee (3-1, 2.1.03) as the Light Blues completed the first half of the programme. Indeed, victory over the Tayside outfit on that freezing January afternoon meant that Rangers headed for their winter break in Dubai three points clear of Celtic at the top of the SPL.

Fast forward to mid-April and the latter stages of the 2002/03 campaign. Despite a truly shocking playing surface at Tannadice, the Dutchman managed to produce an absolutely breathtaking performance (including two goals and an assist) that defied the under foot conditions as Rangers triumphed 4-1. Then, as the SPL race neared a nail-biting climax, de Boer claimed the vital opener against Hearts in Edinburgh, on a day when Rangers just had to collect all three points. On that glorious Sunday in Govan the following week when he hit the twenty goal mark, his second-half header put Rangers 4-1 in front of Dunfermline and back on top of the league table as both halves of the Old Firm pushed for glory.

Following the above Championship Day game, BBC Television named de Boer (club top scorer last season) 'Man of the Match' once again. We rest our case!

dergoalie

Stefan Klos

To say the least, it was rather special and even BBC pundit Gary Lineker agreed that it was, quite simply, one of the saves of the season. Certainly most fans at the Ibrox December 'Old Firm' clash felt that Thompson's shot was net-bound and destined for the top corner before Stefan Klos somehow managed an astonishing fingertip save, preventing a certain goal. In many ways, it just summed up his season.

No one could ever doubt his commitment to Rangers and, despite all his problems with Borussia Dortmund, European Cup medal winner Klos always gave the impression that he would eventually join the Ibrox outfit. After signing for Rangers just before Christmas 1998 (and just two days training with his new companions), the German made his debut in the 1-0 Boxing Day victory over St. Johnstone. On the very last day of that season when Celtic tried in vain to halt the treble juggernaut at Hampden on Scottish Cup final day, he was magnificent and many neutral observers suggested that the 'Man of the Match' award would not have been out of place considering his almost flawless technical display throughout the ninety minutes.

The National stadium was the scene, once again, of yet another truly superb display when Celtic were beaten 2-1 in the February 2002 CIS Insurance Cup semi-final. Klos was in superlative form that famous night with a string of crucial stops to his credit. Indeed, in the first few minutes of the game, two magnificent saves from Petrov and Larsson kept Rangers hopes alive! In the final of that same competition (when Ayr United were Sunday opponents), it was yet another stunning stop when the German somehow managed to claw a McLaughlin chip shot out of the air with the game evenly balanced at 0-0.

In truth, last season was no different with Klos performing wonders on a regular basis. In the Maryhill district of Glasgow, two weeks after that 'Old Firm save from Thompson, he produced the goods yet again with a glorious reflex safe from substitute Scott McLean, denying Partick Thistle a late equaliser. Indeed, when the same outfit travelled to Govan on league duty in early April 2003, Klos prevented his side from falling behind with a trademark 'one on one' stop early in the second period before the Light Blues eventually opened the scoring. Including the latter SPL fixture, the 'keeper had now totalled 203 appearances for Rangers with the team having won148, lost 23 and drawn 32 of the games in question. Additionally, in thirty-eight Premier League fixtures last term, the German achieved nineteen shut-outs.

During the first-half of the penultimate league game of last season (at Gorgie Road, Edinburgh), it was Klos who kept Rangers from going behind with a quite magnificent save from the Hearts Dutch striker Mark de Vries. Then, one week later when Dunfermline were the 2002/03's last visitors, he crucially stopped a powerful Craig Brewster shot in the second period, ensuring that his side's goal difference remained ahead of Celtic's tally as the countdown to glory continued. Often the unsung hero throughout that championship campaign, the goalkeeper was a genuine contender in the 'Player of the Year' stakes last season when he was the only ever-present in the team.

Everybody knows that 'The Goalie' was the legendary Andy Goram. Maybe now, considering his worth to the team, it should simply be 'Der Goalie' instead of Stefan Klos.

king**ofoz**

craig moore

It was an Old Firm encounter that Rangers really needed to win in order to confirm their title aspirations. Prior to the early December Ibrox confrontation last season, the Light Blues were one point adrift at the top of the Scottish Premier League after having played eighteen games. However, with less than one minute on the clock, the required victory seemed a long way off when the lunchtime visitors sensationally took the lead. A quick reply was obviously needed before Celtic could settle on their goal advantage. The answer came from the day's most complete defender when Craig Moore (King of the crunching tackle) powerfully headed home a Fernando Ricksen corner some nine minutes later to level the game.

Oz, it must be said, was more than proficient in his defensive duties throughout the whole campaign and was one of the real contenders for club 'Player of the Year' in Season 2002/03. His year had been quite superb with innumerable timely interceptions and strong defending hallmarks of his game week-in and week-out as Alex McLeish's side grew in strength of character and mind. In addition, his name was on the score sheet in the SPL games with Kilmarnock (6-1, 27.10.02), Dundee (3-0, 2.11.02) and Celtic (as detailed) as well as in the 3-0 Scottish Cup victory over Arbroath in late January 2003.

During the 2002/03 treble period, Craig Moore made more appearances in blue than at any other time in his Rangers career - a total of forty-four starts including the Scottish Cup final on the very last day of May. In truth, when analysing the whole season, it is difficult to remember him having a bad game with reliability being the keyword in his performances.

Surely nothing Moore needs to be said!

RANGERS 6   DUNFERMLINE 1
Mols (3 mins), Caniggia (16), Arveladze (30), de Boer (64)
Thompson (67), Arteta (90)

After thirty-seven league games, Rangers and Celtic could not be separated by points or goal difference at the top of the SPL table and, with just one game remaining, the Ibrox side held the decidedly slim advantage of having scored once more than their Old Firm rivals. All would be decided on the last day of the season when Rangers entertained Dunfermline and Celtic travelled to Rugby Park to face Kilmarnock. In other words, showtime for a showdown!

With just three minutes on the clock, Michael Mols netted the first of the game following a Claudio Caniggia lay-off. After Ronald de Boer had missed a golden opportunity to put Rangers two up almost immediately, Jason Dair struck a glorious drive from twenty-five yards to equalise for the Pars and silence, momentarily, the Ibrox crowd. Then, just after 3.15 pm, the Argentine himself scored (after determined play from Ricksen on the right) before Shota Arveladze's precise header made it three following more determined play but this time from Amoruso wide-left. At half-time, 3-1 Rangers were still on top despite Celtic having ended their own forty-five minutes 2-0 in front.

With Neil McCann on for Caniggia at the start of the second period, Rangers pushed and pushed in search of those vital goals. Then, you could almost feel the tension in the stadium when several hundred radios confirmed that Celtic had taken top-spot after going 3-0 ahead. However, in 64 minutes, Rangers swapped league positions with them when de Boer headed home from McCann's delightful free-kick. Barely two minutes after that, the winger provided again but this time it was Steven Thompson who benefited, netting from very close range for SPL goal number 100 of the league battle. When Neil was subsequently fouled in the box well into injury time, the remarkably composed Mikel Arteta boldly stepped forward to deliver the afternoon's final blow. Stillie was beaten and so indeed were Celtic.

The old stadium had not seen celebrations like it for a very long time but, then again, it's not every day that a world record 50th league championship is realised. And, for the very few that may have forgotten, this was the final reckoning:

	P	W	D	L	F	A	Pts
Rangers	38	31	4	3	101	28	97
Celtic	38	31	4	3	98	26	97

Rangers: Klos, Ricksen, Moore, Amoruso, Numan, Arteta, de Boer, Mols (Thompson) and Caniggia (McCann).

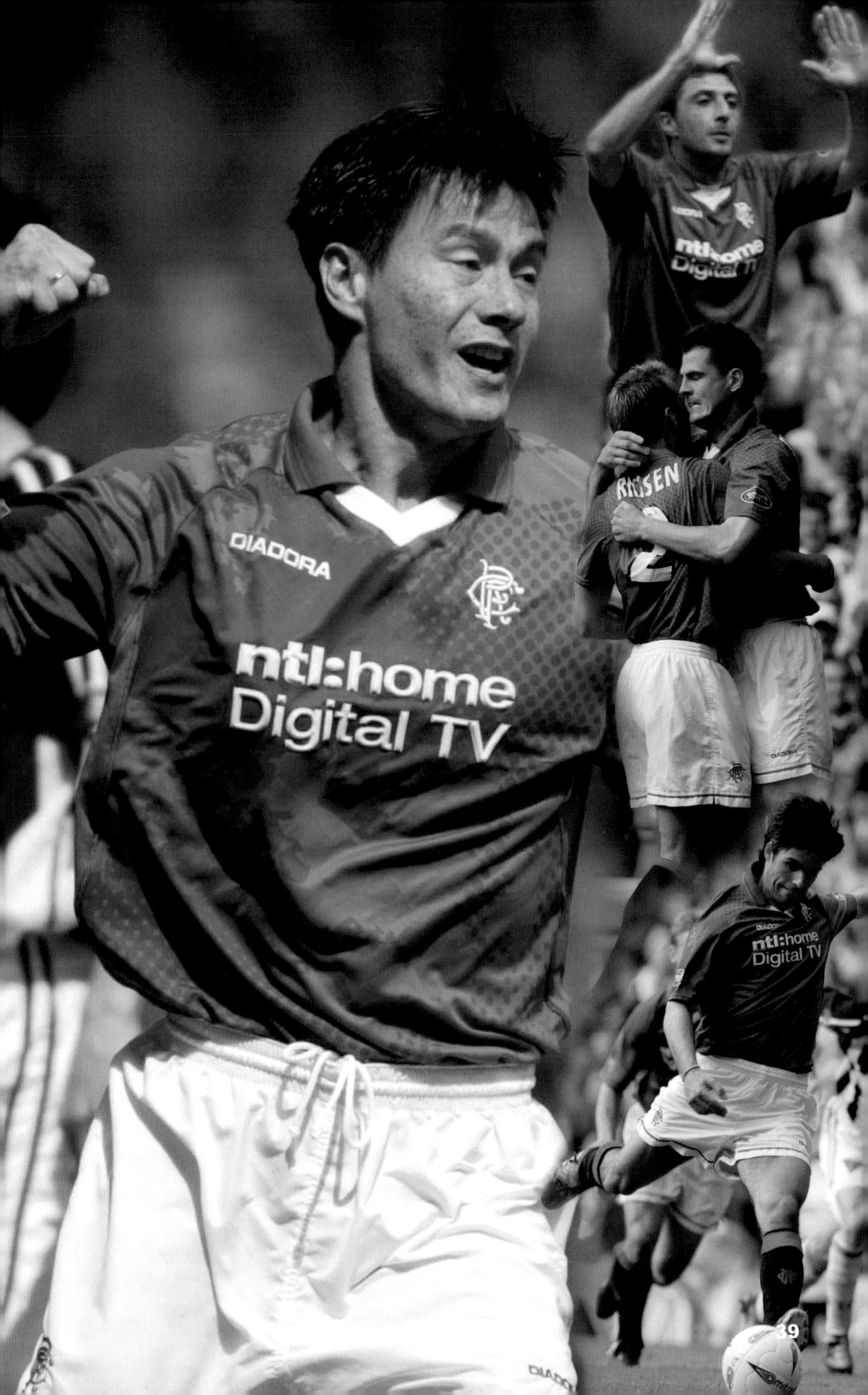
DIADORA
ntl:home
Digital TV

40

stRANGER than fiction

In late 1875, after Rangers had beaten Third Lanarkshire Rifle Volunteers 1-0 in the 2nd round of the Scottish Cup, the SFA declared the match void. Seemingly, Rangers had kicked-off at the start of each half! Following a 2-1 defeat in the replay (which was abandoned several minutes before the end of normal time due to fans on the pitch), Rangers protested to the SFA that, in addition to ninety minutes not being played, the Third Lanark goalkeeper could not be distinguished from the fans directly behind his goal (as he too was wearing street clothes) and that a hand was used to score their first goal. The SFA rejected their appeal, the result stood and Rangers were out of the cup.

At the start of Season 1906/07, Celtic provided the opposition in a benefit game for Rangers' left-sided forward Finlay Speedie who had signed for Newcastle United. During this encounter, Celtic goalkeeper Adams badly injured his hand on a rough nail at Ibrox and, because their Old Firm rivals had no cover in this position, Rangers offered the temporary services of their reserve 'keeper Tom Sinclair. By keeping clean sheets in his first six Celtic league games, he created a record that was unequalled at the club until 1994. By the time Sinclair returned to Ibrox after his temporary Parkhead stay, he was the proud owner of a Glasgow Cup medal …won with Celtic!

The first post war Rangers player to break the 100 goal barrier was Willie Thornton. The legendary centre-forward, who won the Military Medal in Sicily in 1943 during the Second World War, was never booked or sent-off in his entire playing career. In later years, between the Davie White/Willie Waddell management periods, he had a brief spell in charge at Ibrox. Taking control of the team for two winning matches, Willie Thornton is the only Rangers' manager in history with, therefore, a 100% record!

The club's greatest domestic goal-scoring feat of the 20th Century was against the minnows of Blairgowrie in the Scottish Cup campaign of Season 1933/34. A home crowd of just 5000 saw Jimmy Fleming net an astonishing nine times in a record 14-2 victory - with the final four Rangers goals coming in the last four minutes of the game. The Ibrox side would go on to complete a domestic clean sweep that season by winning not only this trophy (St. Mirren were crushed 5-0 in the final) but also the League Championship, the Glasgow Cup and the Glasgow Charity Cup.

The very first 'Old Firm' Ne'erday game was played at Celtic Park in January 1898. After some seventy minutes with the score tied at 1-1, (and Rangers pushing for the required winner to close the gap at the top of the league table), the referee abandoned the game following a pitch invasion. Although Celtic were blamed for the incident as they had only 'employed' some 40 policemen for crowd control purposes, the club were having none of it, suggesting instead that responsibility must remain with the trouble-makers in the crowd. Rangers were annoyed when they received only 20% of the gate receipts after being under the impression that an equal 50/50 split agreement had been made between the two clubs in advance of the game!

stRANGER than fiction?

When Hibernian won 3-2 at Ibrox in the Scottish Cup campaign of Season 1895/96, it was the first time that the Edinburgh side had faced the Light Blues in any cup competition. Despite knowing that his side had missed two penalties, Rangers goalkeeper John Bell accepted full responsibility for the defeat. After the final whistle, he made his way to the dressing room, changed in silence and, without saying a word to any of the team, walked out of the ground for the very last time. Bell never ever returned to Ibrox!

Following a first-round victory over Monaco in the European Cup of Season 1961/62, Rangers were paired with East German champions Vorwaerts of Berlin. In those days, Germany's major city was still divided and the Berlin Wall a very real and frightening reminder of the deep distrust that existed between East and West. A week after securing a precious 2-1 away victory, manager Scot Symon was forced to take his team to Malmo in Sweden for the home fixture since, due to the rampant paranoia of the time, it was impossible for the Vorwaerts squad to obtain visas to any NATO country. Obviously, Sweden was not a member of NATO. With Rangers 1-0 ahead, the game was abandoned at half-time because of dense November fog and rescheduled for a next day kick-off. The following morning, a pre-noon crowd of just 1781 (mainly Rangers fans) witnessed progress to the next round after a comfortable 4-1 win.

stRANGER than fiction?

In Season 1898/99, Rangers not only achieved championship glory but also created a world record by winning every single league game that year. With an amazing average of more than four goals per game, the Light Blues inflicted crushing defeats on teams such as Clyde (8-0), Dundee (7-0) and Partick Thistle (5-0) as well as 4-0 and 4-1 triumphs over Celtic. In addition, that other team in green Hibernian were also soundly beaten but their suffering was on an even greater scale. It may be hard to believe but, at Ibrox on Christmas Eve, Rangers crushed their Edinburgh rivals 10-0!

There and then were 3

The Scottish Cup Campaign of 2003

ARBROATH 0 RANGERS 3

Rangers began the defence of their trophy against First Division Arbroath at a bitterly cold Gayfield Park in late January. Barry Ferguson, who had struck the bar right at the start, claimed his side's first of the night with a left-foot beauty from all of twenty yards after some twenty-six minutes played. Almost immediately, Craig Moore effectively killed the game with a powerful penalty-box header (following Fernando Ricksen's corner) and completely silenced the home support whose earlier chants of 'Are You Montrose In Disguise?' certainly raised a smile or two in the freezing East coast wind. After the gloved Shota Arveladze had made it three in the second-half and completed the scoring, thoughts turned from east to west coast and Rangers next port of call down in Ayrshire.

Rangers: Klos, Ross, Moore, Amoruso (Malcolm), Numan, Ricksen, Ferguson, De Boer, Mols, Arveladze (McLean) and McCann (Caniggia).

AYR UNITED 0 RANGERS 1

On a far from perfect Somerset Park playing surface, Campbell Money's young Ayr United side ensured that this was no seaside stroll for Rangers although, in truth, the Ibrox club, had numerous chances to win this fourth-round encounter with both Arveladze (a fierce shot off the bar) and Stephen Hughes (four efforts on goal) coming close before the eventual, late winner. The crucial, deciding strike finally arrived deep into the second-half when, following substitute Steven Thompson's cross, Ronald de Boer rose perfectly to head home past the wrong-footed Nelson between the posts. All's well that ends well and Rangers, again drawn away from home, would now face SPL quarter-final opposition in the shape of Dunfermline at East End Park.

Rangers: Klos, Muscat, Moore, Amoruso, Numan, Ferguson, Malcolm (Thompson), Arteta (Hughes), Arveladze, De Boer and McCann (Caniggia).

DUNFERMLINE 1 RANGERS 1

Frenchman David Grondin (a former Arsenal reserve) gave his side the lead midway through the first-half before Claudio Caniggia slid home following a delightful through ball from de Boer and equalised for Rangers just eight minutes later. The Argentine striker had now netted six times at East End Park in Season 2002/03. Rangers continued to create chances throughout the game but, once again, failed to convert those chances into goals. Late-on, both Arveladze and Caniggia missed with headers that on other occasions would surely have ended up in the back of the net and then, right at the end, Barry Ferguson was dismissed following an ill-advised lunge at substitute Hunt. The Fifers now travelled to Ibrox for the replay, no doubt in the knowledge that the last time a Dunfermline team won in Govan was thirty-one years previously, back in 1972!

Rangers: Klos, Muscat, Moore, Malcolm, Ricksen, Ferguson, Arteta, Caniggia, De Boer and McCann (Arveladze).

RANGERS 3 DUNFERMLINE 0

Partly due to live television coverage, a disappointing crowd of less than 25,000 gathered at Ibrox for the April replay. Rangers began well and, with only four minutes on the stadium clock, Peter Lovenkrands netted his eleventh goal of the season to put the 'Light Blues' ahead. In eighteen minutes, with a diving header, it was number eighteen of Barry Ferguson's season with Arthur Numan (back after several weeks on the injury list) the provider. Rangers were controlling the game and the one-way traffic continued in the direction of Stillie for much of the remaining first-half. Mikel Arteta, with his first since scoring on his Celtic Park debut back in October, made it three early in the second period with a delightful chip that fooled both 'keeper and a couple of defenders. The final whistle confirmed that Alex McLeish would be taking his side back to the National Stadium for the seventh time since arriving at the club.

Rangers: Klos, Ricksen, Amoruso, Numan (McCann), Arteta, Konterman, Ferguson, De Boer (Caniggia), Mols and Lovenkrands.

There were 3
and then
The Scottish Cup Campaign of 2003

SEMI-FINAL
MOTHERWELL 3 RANGERS 4

Many felt that Rangers would go on to win this semi-final clash with ease after Bert Konterman's beautifully struck shot from just outside the box gave them a goal of a start in just two minutes. Terry Butcher's young side had other ideas however and the SPL strugglers hit back twice to take a 2-1 lead at the break. Indeed, Rangers could have faced an even greater second-half fight if David Clarkson had not missed a clear chance just before the end of that first period! With Steven Thompson on for Arveladze, the game swung Rangers' way and, after Barry Ferguson struck the bar from twenty-five yards, Michael Mols netted from a sweet Thompson pass to square the game in fifty-six minutes. Then, almost immediately, Amoruso rose quite majestically above the Motherwell rearguard to power home from a Ricksen corner. A Partridge own-goal finally killed the tie although Motherwell did get a little, late consolation courtesy of Adams. Rangers were through to their fourth consecutive Hampden final in a row.

Rangers: Klos, Muscat, Amoruso, Moore (Malcolm), Numan, Ricksen (Hughes), Ferguson, Konterman, Arveladze (Thompson), Mols and McCann.

SCOTTISH CUP FINAL
DUNDEE 0 RANGERS 1

After the high anxiety of the previous week's SPL title decider, it was maybe inevitable that this game (played in Seville-like hot, humid conditions) was a less dramatic encounter with neither side dominating proceedings. After Dundee's Barry Smith had rattled the left-hand post of Stefan Klos early on, Michael Mols, later in that same first-half, returned the compliment with a header (from Neil McCann's free-kick) that rebounded off the bar. The only goal of the game came midway through the second period when Lorenzo Amoruso headed home from another McCann free-kick. After all the media speculation surrounding his future, maybe it was appropriate that the Italian's name should be on the winner. Certainly his tears, following the final whistle, had a powerful effect on many of the Ibrox legions that day. For the seventh time in their proud history, Rangers had won all three domestic trophies in the same astonishingly brilliant season.

Rangers: Klos, Ricksen, Moore, Amoruso, Numan (Muscat), Malcolm, Arveladze (Thompson), Ferguson, McCann, Mols (Ross) and de Boer.

TENNENT'S SCOTTISH CUP
FINAL 2002-2003

46

rangers

1. Rangers were drawn away to which SPL club when they entered the competition at the third round stage?

2. What was the score and who netted the late winner for Rangers?

3. Name the player injured during the warm-up who had to be replaced before kick-off?

4. Where was Rangers next port of call in the tournament?

5. Who came off the bench to net a late winner in this game?

6. Name the opponents in what turned out to be a rather dour semi-final clash.

7. Ronald de Boer scored the only goal of the game. True or false?

8. Who scored for Rangers against Celtic in the final?

9. What unusual feat was claimed by the scorer of the Light Blues winning goal?

10. How many times have Rangers now won the League Cup competition?

Answers on page 63

look for the
silverlining

RANGERS 2   CELTIC 1

Caniggia (23 mins)   Larsson (56 mins)
Lovenkrands (34 mins)

Prior to this Hampden meeting to contest the first silverware of the season, many neutral observers felt that Celtic held the psychological advantage. After all, the Parkhead side had defeated the league leaders in the championship race the previous week, closing the gap to just three points at the top of the SPL table with Celtic a game in hand. Today, however, the circumstances were entirely different and the 'follow-followers' knew that Alex McLeish's side would be more than determined to retain the trophy after an admitted poor showing only days earlier in the east end of Glasgow.

Certainly Ranger's path to the final had not been littered with easy games. In the third round of the tournament, the holders faced stiff competition when they travelled to Easter Road before disposing of Hibernian 3-2 despite going behind after just six minutes. Then it was over the Forth to Fife (and Dunfermline at East End Park) where substitute Claudio Caniggia's late headed winner set up a Hampden semi-final date with Hearts. In a dour, bad-tempered game, Ronald de Boer's first-half header saw resolute Rangers through to another Hampden date. Celtic, on the other hand, had a somewhat easier set of home games (Inverness Cal. Thistle and Partick Thistle) prior to Dundee United at the penultimate, neutral stage of the contest.

At the National Stadium that mid-March afternoon, Rangers could have gone ahead as early as minute thirteen of the final when a Peter Lovenkrands effort (following a long Jerome Bonnissel ball down the left-hand side) was cleared off the line by defender

Valgaeren with 'keeper Douglas beaten. Those of a blue persuasion, however, did not have long to wait before saluting the game's opening goal when Claudio Caniggia netted some ten minutes later. Once again, the Dane Lovenkrands was to the fore as his pass inside, after cutting in from the left, was converted quite simply by the Argentine from close-in (despite Balde's attempted block) after Michael Mols had just failed to make contact himself.

Then, with just over half-an-hour gone, the holders doubled their tally with a quite delightful strike. Bonnissel and Mols were both involved once again before the Dutch master played a super through ball to Lovenkrands whose sure-footed strike left Douglas without a Hampden hope. Despite Larsson twice coming close before the break, it remained at 2-0 for the holders after forty-five minutes play. Understandably, Celtic pressed hard right from the start of the second period and eventually got their reward when Larsson scored with just over thirty minutes remaining. Although the Light Blues held firm after that, it looked as if the game could possibly go into extra-time when Celtic were awarded a penalty right at the death following an Amoruso challenge in the box. However, Hartson's spot-kick was wide and his team was beaten.

After the previous week's disappointment in the east end of the city, the Ibrox side had answered their critics in the best possible fashion and the name of Rangers would now grace the trophy for a record twenty-third time. To all those friends of Rangers in the Hampden sun, it certainly was a beautiful day.

oldfirm QUIZ
SEASON 2002/03

1. What was the score in the first Old Firm clash of the season?

2. Who claimed the opening goal that day?

3. Who played the ninety minutes with a broken nose?

4. In the December Ibrox clash, who netted the crucial early equaliser?

5. Who scored the winner that Saturday lunchtime?

6. At that stage of his Rangers career, manager Alex McLeish was now undefeated in _____ clashes with Martin O'Neill. Fill in the missing number.

7. Whose thunderous free-kick came close to salvaging a point at Celtic Park in early March?

8. What happened the week after the above 1-0 SPL defeat?

9. Who scored for Rangers in the final Old Firm clash of the season?

10. How many times have Rangers now won the league championship compared to Celtic?

Answers on page 63

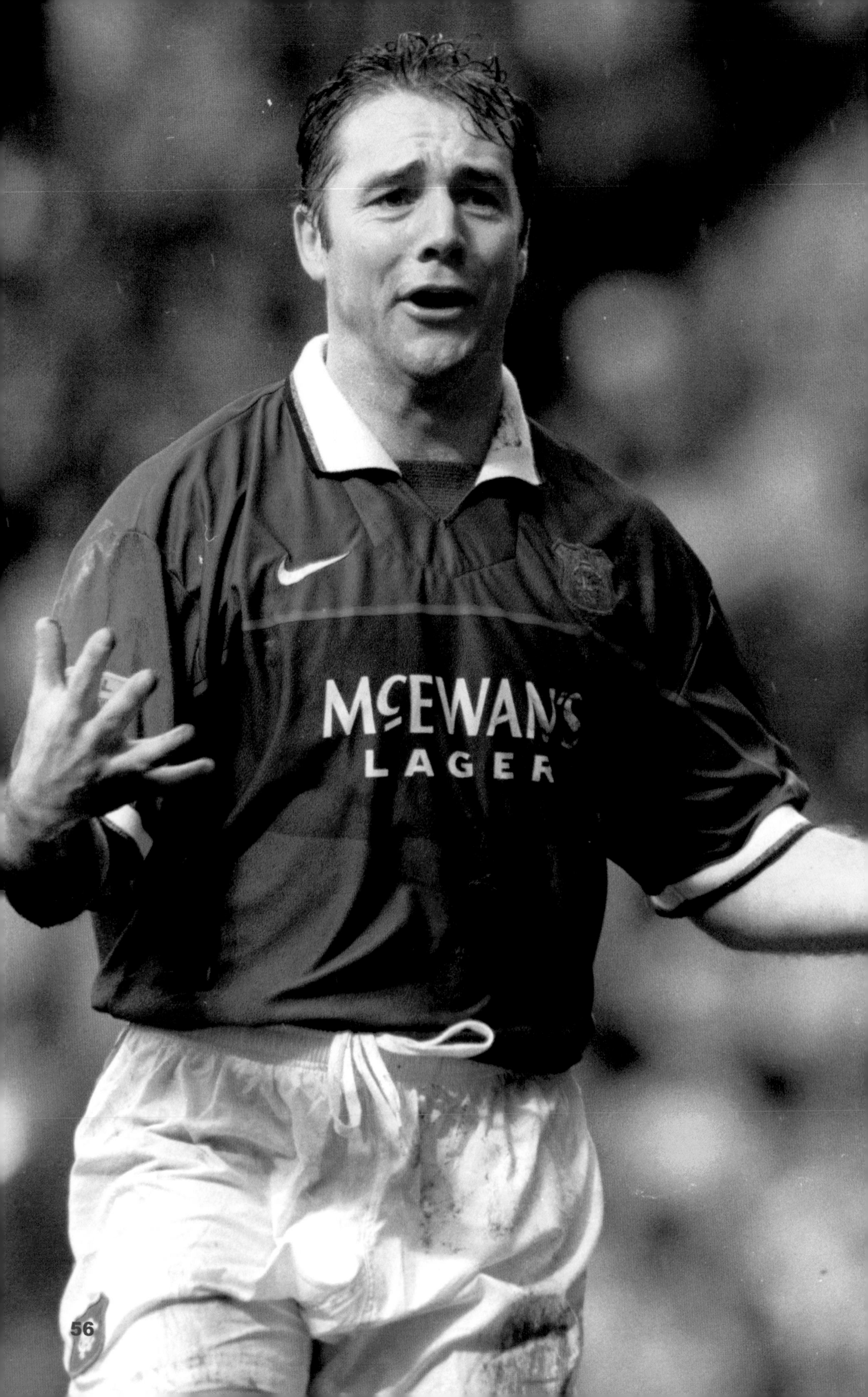
McEWAN'S
LAGER

in a⁹row

With memories of the club's 2003 SPL Championship still fresh in the mind, let's re-visit that astonishing period from Season 1988/1989 to Season 1996/1997 when Rangers claimed nine league championships in a row.

SEASON 1988/89	P	W	D	L	F	A	Pts
Rangers	36	26	4	6	62	26	56
Aberdeen	36	18	14	4	51	25	50
Celtic	36	11	14	11	66	44	46

Defender Gary Stevens (from Everton) and striker Kevin Drinkell (from Norwich City) both joined Rangers for the start of the campaign along with captain Terry Butcher who returned after a leg break sustained the previous November. The season included 5-1 and 4-1 thrashings of Celtic (as well as a crucial 2-1 Pittodrie victory over close rivals Aberdeen in mid-January) before Graeme Souness' side finally secured the championship at Ibrox in late April when Hearts were beaten 4-0, courtesy of doubles by both Drinkell and Mel Sterland. Prior to that game, Rangers had won 11 of their previous 13 league matches on the road to glory.

SEASON 1989/90	P	W	D	L	F	A	Pts
Rangers	36	20	11	5	48	19	51
Aberdeen	36	17	10	9	56	33	44
Hearts	36	16	12	8	54	35	44

The cultured Trevor Steven signed from Everton and ex-Celt Maurice Johnston arrived (somewhat sensationally to say the least!) from Nantes. Both of these new signings would become major players for the club as Rangers, despite losing their opening two league encounters, retained the championship for the first time since 1976. By season's end, Johnston had become top scorer in the league with 15 goals, the most famous of which was surely his late, late winner when Celtic were beaten 1-0 at Ibrox in November. Incidentally, when Rangers recorded the same score at Celtic park in early January, it was the Light Blues' first 'Ne'erday' win at this ground in over twenty years! Midfielder Trevor Steven netted the title-winning goal against Dundee United at Tannadice in April.

SEASON 1990/91	P	W	D	L	F	A	Pts
Rangers	36	24	7	5	62	23	55
Aberdeen	36	22	9	5	62	27	53
Celtic	36	17	7	12	52	38	41

Arriving from Monaco, striker Mark Hateley did not exactly receive the warmest of welcomes from some fans when he first wore the blue of Rangers. However, by the end of his first year at the club, the player had virtually achieved legendary status. In many ways, it was a difficult time in Govan – early-on in the season, Terry Butcher left the club under controversial circumstances, injuries to key players such as Richard Gough, Ian Ferguson, Ally McCoist and Trevor Steven disturbed the team pattern and, in April, Graeme Souness returned to Liverpool as manager at a time when the championship was still in the balance. On the last day of league campaign, with Walter Smith now in charge, Aberdeen required only a draw with Rangers to claim the title. However, on one of the most dramatic Ibrox occasions for many a long year, two Hateley goals meant that the Light Blues lifted a third consecutive title for the first time since 1945.

in a⁹row

SEASON 1991/92							
	P	W	D	L	F	A	Pts
Rangers	44	33	6	5	101	31	72
Hearts	44	27	9	8	60	37	63
Celtic	44	26	10	8	88	42	62

Two new faces were goalkeeper Andy Goram (simply 'The Goalie' in due course) and midfielder Stuart McCall who joined from Hibernian and Everton respectively as the champions began their title defence with a 6-0 triumph over St. Johnstone in early August. Ally Super netted 34 times that season. As well as becoming the first Scot to win Europe's 'Golden Boot' trophy, the striker claimed his 200th Scottish league goal away to Aberdeen in early May. In total, Rangers had buried an astonishing 101 goals in 44 domestic league games. Certainly victory in 19 out of 22 away games went a long way to securing a fourth successive championship – for the first time in over 60 years! Incidentally, this period would also bear fruit to the club's first League and Scottish Cup double since 1978 following victory over Airdrie on the last day of the season at Hampden.

SEASON 1992/93							
	P	W	D	L	F	A	Pts
Rangers	44	33	7	4	97	35	73
Aberdeen	44	27	10	7	87	36	64
Celtic	44	24	12	8	68	41	60

After losing to Dundee at Dens Park in mid-August, Rangers showed remarkable consistency and were beaten in only one championship game before securing the league title in Airdrie at the beginning of May the following year. Two players were responsible for 65 of the team's 97 goals - Ally McCoist (another special season for him) equalled his previous year's tally of 44 and Mark Hateley (by now a true blue Warrior King) contributed greatly with 21 of his own. Rangers also won their first treble (and the fifth in the club's history) since the days of manager Jock Wallace back in 1977/78 in addition to embarking on the most wonderful European run. A series of 10 unbeaten Champions' Cup games took the Blues Brothers so close to the final of the European Cup for the very first time. It was one of those seasons when everyone was a hero.

SEASON 1993/94							
	P	W	D	L	F	A	Pts
Rangers	44	22	14	8	74	41	58
Aberdeen	44	17	21	6	58	36	55
Motherwell	44	20	14	10	58	43	54

With Celtic conspicuous by their absence in the top three, it had been the somewhat unlikely duo of Aberdeen and Motherwell that offered the strongest championship challenge that season. Indeed, the Fir Park outfit defeated Rangers both home and away before the defending champions (despite losing the likes of Goram and McCoist for much of the campaign) made it six-in-a-row. Top scorer Mark Hateley hit 22 goals and became the first Englishman to be named 'Player of the Year' by the Scottish Football Writers' Association. In a memorable 'Ne'erday' clash at Celtic Park, the visitors struck like a hurricane and were 3-0 ahead after just half an hour's play! The final 4-2 victory was achieved with goals from Hateley, Mikhailitchenko and Kuznetsov – an Englishman and two Ukrainians!

in a row

SEASON 1994/95	P	W	D	L	F	A	Pts
Rangers	36	20	9	7	60	35	69
Motherwell	36	14	12	10	50	50	54
Hibernian	36	12	17	7	49	37	53

Season 1994/95 saw the Glasgow arrival of Dane Brian Laudrup (an absolute steal at £2.25million from Fiorentina!) who would take his place in the Ibrox hall of fame as one of the most talented footballers ever to wear Rangers blue. When Rangers defeated Celtic 3-1 in the league at Hampden in October (Celtic Park was being rebuilt), Laudrup's goal that afternoon was considered by many to be one of the best of the whole campaign. In total, he would net ten times in the 1994/95 period, three short of top scorer Mark Hateley's thirteen strikes in the championship race. Alex McLeish's Motherwell side finished runners-up in the league and Celtic, for the seventh year in succession, finished outside the top two.

SEASON 1995/96	P	W	D	L	F	A	Pts
Rangers	36	27	6	3	85	25	87
Celtic	36	24	11	1	74	25	83
Aberdeen	36	16	7	13	52	45	55

Paul Gascoigne entered the 1995/96 arena and bleach blonde hair was once again in vogue down Ibrox way! The 'Old Firm' meetings were particularly important that season with a rejuvenated Celtic pushing Rangers all the way. Three of the four Rangers/Celtic clashes were drawn, with the Light Blues victorious in the other fixture which was the Parkhead side's only defeat in the title race. In that crucial encounter, goals from full-back Alex Cleland (with a header) and Gascoigne (running virtually the length of the park before netting a McCoist pass for one of the gems of the season) sealed the points. It was the Geordie lad himself who grabbed all the headlines in April when his astonishing hat-trick against Aberdeen finally secured the championship crown for Rangers. Three weeks later at the National Stadium, a crushing 5-1 Scottish Cup final defeat of Hearts meant a domestic double.

SEASON 1996/97	P	W	D	L	F	A	Pts
Rangers	36	25	5	6	85	33	80
Celtic	36	23	6	7	78	32	75
Dundee Utd	36	17	9	10	46	33	60

The final piece of the 'nine' jigsaw was put in place at Tannadice on 7 May 1997. With a rare headed goal (his last was for Fiorentina in the game with Roma), Brian Laudrup secured a 1-0 victory for Rangers ....and the celebrations began. It was entirely fitting that the Dane's goal should secure the championship as, once again, his contribution had been quite immense. Not surprisingly, for the second time in just three seasons, the Scottish Football Writers' Association named him Player of the Year a short time later. Another 1-0 victory, but this time in the east end of Glasgow in March, had earlier ended Celtic's faint hope of stopping the Rangers juggernaut.

When the first of the sequence had been realised back in April 1989, another eight consecutive championships seemed nothing more than an impossible dream. By May 1997, however, that dream had become reality.

1. Who scored Rangers first and last goals of the SPL season?

2. Name the first player to claim a hat-trick in the league campaign?

3. How many times did the Light Blues hit five or more goals?

4. Following which victory did Rangers take top spot in the table?

5. Prior to the late December defeat at Motherwell, how many SPL goals had Rangers netted that same month?

6. Apart from Celtic, name the other two sides to attract a crowd of over 49,000 for both Ibrox visits.

7. What was out of character for Barry Ferguson at Dens Park in early May?

8. Barry Ferguson never managed a hat-trick in any SPL encounter. True or false?

9. With less than ten minutes on the clock, whose two clinical strikes against Kilmarnock at Ibrox in the penultimate home game of the season set Rangers on the road to a crucial victory?

10. Name the scorers on Championship Day at Ibrox in late May 2003.

Answers on page 63

the quotes
who said that? QUIZ

1. "Quite often, first impressions last and I think that was the case with him. When his name was put forward to me by an agent, I nearly bit his hand off."

2. "Stefan Klos did well for Rangers. He made some good saves and the one from Alan Thompson was one of the saves of the season for me."

3. "I thought I was going to have to buy a ticket to get back into the stadium. If that was him just coming back, I don't want to play against him when he's on fire."

4. "He has a heart of gold and is willing to help everyone throughout the club, so you won't hear anyone say a bad word against him."

5. "The chance came out of the blue sky. Steven delivered a great cross but it was an even better header."

6. "My grandfather was a Rangers fan, really passionate about the team, a man who went to every match, with out wearing a scarf, without singing any songs, but who still religiously followed Rangers."

7. "Ally comes from the same village as me, Houston, and I know him from there. I spoke to him at half-time and he wished me all the best."

8. "Rangers changed things at half-time and steamrollered us after that. Steven Thompson made a big difference. They stepped up a gear and blew us away."

9. "I thought we were brilliant for the first five seconds."

10. "I never sign anybody who's quite a bit healthier looking in the shower than I am."

Answers on page 63

QUIZ
ANSWERS

HEADLINE NEWS

1. Ronald de Boer's winner in the Scottish Cup tie at Ayr.
2. Motherwell push Rangers all the way in the Scottish Cup semi-final.
3. Claudio Caniggia's goal in the 2-0 win over Hearts helps Rangers to top spot in the SPL.
4. Barry Ferguson impressive once again, this time in 1-0 win over Hearts.
5. Craig Moore speaking about Lorenzo Amoruso after the Scottish Cup final.
6. Rangers 3-0 Scottish Cup win on an extremely windy Arbroath evening.
7. With goal difference still a possibility in deciding the Championship, Rangers score four against Kilmarnock but created chances enough to double that number.
8. Barry Ferguson is named Player of the Year by the Scottish Football Writers' Association.
9. Mikel Arteta's final minute penalty and the 2003 SPL title.
10. Alex McLeish becomes the sixth Rangers manager to achieve the domestic treble.

MISSING WORD QUIZ

1. McLeish (unbeaten at Hampden in eight Rangers visits)
2. Mols (Michael's winning goal in the 3-2 SPL victory over Celtic)
3. Lovenkrands (1-0 Rugby Park victory)
4. Moore (following the defender's superb display in 3-0 Dens Park win)
5. Ricksen (Bank of Scotland 'Player of the Month' for October 2002)
6. De Boer (ref. his superb display and goals in the 4-1 Tannadice victory)
7. Maurice (Ross claims his first-ever Rangers goal in the 2-0 Livingston victory)
8. Barry (reputed amount of Barry Ferguson's new five-year contract)
9. Thompson (Steven Thompson scores against Dundee on his Rangers debut)
10. De Boer (Ronald's crucial opener against Hearts in the penultimate SPL clash)

SCOTTISH CUP QUIZ

1. Arbroath.
2. Barry Ferguson, Craig Moore and Shota Arveladze in the 3-0 win.
3. Somerset Park.
4. False – it was Ronald de Boer.
5. Claudio Caniggia.
6. Barry Ferguson.
7. Barry Ferguson.
8. 2-1 to Motherwell.
9. Lorenzo Amoruso.
10. Maurice Ross, Steven Thompson and Kevin Muscat.

1. Hibernian.
2. 3-2, Peter Lovenkrands.
3. Lorenzo Amoruso.
4. Dunfermline.
5. Claudio Caniggia.
6. Hearts.
7. True.
8. Claudio Caniggia and Peter Lovenkrands.
9. Peter Lovenkrands had now scored the winner in the last two Hampden cup finals against Celtic.
10. A record 23 times.

SEASON 2002/03 OLD FIRM QUIZ

1. A 3-3 draw.
2. Mikel Arteta.
3. Lorenzo Amoruso.
4. Craig Moore.
5. Michael Mols.
6. Six.
7. Lorenzo Amoruso.
8. Rangers beat Celtic 2-1 in the CIS Insurance Cup final.
9. Ronald de Boer.
10. 50 wins compared to Celtic's 38 wins.

ONE IN A ROW QUIZ

1. Shota Arveladze and Mikel Arteta.
2. Claudio Caniggia in the 6-0 September defeat of Dunfermline.
3. Three times – in the 6-0/6-1 victories over Dunfermline and the 6-1 beating of Kilmarnock.
4. Hearts, 11.9.02.
5. 16 in 5 games.
6. Aberdeen and Motherwell.
7. He failed to score with either of two penalties!
8. False – he netted three times in the 3-0 December win over Dundee United.
9. Michael Mols.
10. Mols (2), Caniggia, Arveladze, de Boer, Thompson and Arteta.

THE QUOTES QUIZ

1. Alex McLeish speaking about the signing of Nuno Capucho.
2. BBC's Gary Lineker after the December 2002 'Old Firm' clash.
3. Dunfermline defender Scott Wilson after a Michael Mols master-class in the November 2002 Ibrox game.
4. Craig Moore speaking about Lorenzo Amoruso after the Scottish Cup final.
5. Ronald de Boer again and his winning goal in the February 2003 Scottish Cup tie with Ayr.
6. Former Rangers manager Walter Smith interviewed before the March 2003 'Old Firm' game.
7. Speaking about Ally McCoist, Steven Thompson after his goal-scoring debut in the January 2003 win over Dundee.
8. Motherwell manager Terry Butcher whose team led at half-time but were eventually beaten 4-3 in the Scottish Cup semi-final of 19.4.03.
9. Kilmarnock manager Jim Jefferies after his team's comprehensive 4-0 defeat at Ibrox in early May.
10. Dundee manager Jim Duffy after the Scottish Cup final when asked about an Amoruso/ Khizanishvili swap deal